Ali Aslam's

Shish Mahal

Cook Book

compiled by
FLLOYD KENNEDY

ALLOWAY PUBLISHING, AYR

TO THE GENEROUS HEARTED PEOPLE
OF GLASGOW

This book is dedicated by Ali Aslam of the Shish
Mahal Restaurant as a contribution to the
community which has supported it over the years.

The proceeds will go to the appeal for the Prince
and Princess of Wales Hospice, which is Glasgow's
wedding gift to the Royal Couple.

Shish Mahal

In 1961, Mr N. Mohammed opened the Greengate Asian Restaurant. It was the first Pakistani restaurant in Glasgow. Mr Mohammed soon introduced his son Ali to the secrets of the kitchen, and they opened the Shish Mahal restaurant in 1964. Starting with only five tables, the restaurant was gradually extended, and today 110 people can be seated.

The restaurant takes its name from the 300 year old 'Mirror Palace' of Lahore, in the North Punjab region of Pakistan. Built by two of the great Moghul emperors, the original Shish Mahal features thousands of beautifully coloured convex mirrors, and in certain chambers, fountains cascade over cunningly arranged lamps.

As a family business, the Shish Mahal restaurant is still under the personal direction of Ali and his brother Nasim, and they and their staff are delighted to give advice on the various dishes available.

The restaurant is unlicensed by choice, but Ali is happy to serve drinks brought by customers, with no corkage charge.

First Published in 1982
by
Alloway Publishing Ltd.,
Ayr.

Reprinted
1982
1983
1984
1985
1986
1987
1989
1992

Printed in Scotland
by
Walker & Connell Ltd.,
Hastings Square, Darvel,
Ayrshire.

ISBN No. 0 907526 08 X

City Chambers Glasgow G2 1DU

From the Lord Provost

Foreword from The Rt. Hon. The Lord Provost
Michael Kelly, JP, BSc(Econ), PhD

As a Patron of the Shish Mahal for many years I have often wished that I could recreate some of the splendid aromas and tastes for which that restaurant is famous.

I have managed to secure one closely-guarded recipe and have been able to serve up a genuine chicken curry to guests to my home.

This book will enable me to expand my repertoire and allow me to extend what culinary talents I have.

Pakistani food is so popular in Scotland that I am sure these recipes will find a place in most kitchens in the City.

The book is well worth purchasing for its own sake but the fact that the entire proceeds from its sale go to the Prince and Princess of Wales Hospice makes it doubly welcome.

A final word; the one thing that a good curry in Glasgow lacks is proper beverage to accompany it. Alcohol doesn't mix with Pakistani food and aerated drinks merely destroy the food's flavour. In San Francisco I discovered that there was an ideal drink. It is called Lassi and the recipe for it is on page 19.

Insist on it when you go out for your next curry!

Michael Kelly

INTRODUCTION

To enable the reader to reproduce as closely as possible the dishes of the Shish Mahal, Ali has recruited Flloyd Kennedy to adapt the recipes for use at home.

The recipes were created for a large establishment, and close co-operation has been necessary to re-create them in a normal domestic kitchen. Sophisticated catering equipment and expert supervision provide the restaurant with a consistency rarely enjoyed by the do-it-yourself gourmet, who may be required to deal with the needs of small children while preparing the rice.

The limited facilities available to the adventurous home cook have been taken into account, and information has been included to assist those wishing to experiment with spices to create their own variations. Although each recipe is complete in itself, browsing through the book at leisure should give a deeper understanding of the techniques involved, and everyone who tries them out will have a better understanding of the skill and dedication that the restaurant provides for its customers.

Mr ALI ASLAM

S
H
I
S
H

M
A
H
A
L

C
O
O
K

B
O
O
K

C
O
N
T
E
N
T
S

THE SPICES

From the ancient times, spices have been sought for their magical, mystical and medicinal powers, and also to preserve and season food.

Magellan died in his search for spices, but his expedition was the first to circumnavigate the world. Of the five ships that set out, only one returned, but it did so in triumph as it was laden with cloves.

Nowadays, the use of spices is mainly confined to their seasoning function, although the colour they provide also plays an important part in the preparation of many dishes.

Spices do not last forever. Their shelf life is strictly limited, and it is this fact which is responsible for many a lack-lustre meal finding its way to the dining table. Powdered spices in particular lose their flavour gradually, even in airtight containers, so if your spice rack contains jars or packets which are approaching 12 months of age, do yourself and your palate a favour, and toss them out!

Whole spices, on the other hand, are less expensive, and much easier to control. For one thing, using whole spices in your cooking will add a new dimension — that of texture. Secondly, if you have all the individual spices to hand you can copy a recipe exactly, and then vary it to your own taste. A little more clove here, a little less cummin there, will not make a disastrous difference, but it will make your cooking uniquely your own.

Most Indian and Pakistani grocers keep a good stock of whole spices, and as they will have a quick turnover of stock the products will be fresh.

CARDAMOM: The cardamom is the seed pod of a member of the ginger family. There are several kinds, ranging from pale green to dark brown in colour, or bleached white. The cardamom, with its warm, lemony flavour, is found in most masalas, and often the small black seeds are removed from the pod, then crushed and ground.

CHILLI: The ingredient that gives the distinctive 'hot' quality to Indo/Pak dishes. When fresh they are either green or red, and can be purchased fairly easily now in most Asian grocers, and supermarkets. They can also be bought in dried and ground form. When handling chillies, take care to keep them — and your fingers — away from the face; and note that the seeds are much hotter than the flesh.

CINNAMON: The dried inner bark of an evergreen tree which is rolled into sticks from about 3" to 8" in length. Fairly aromatic, and useful in both sweet and savoury dishes.

CLOVES: Known to the westerner for their preservative qualities, the warm, sweet smell of cloves adds much to Indian cooking, particularly to the Pulaos and other rice dishes. Oil of cloves is a much used remedy for toothache.

CORIANDER: The aromatic green leaves of this plant are chopped and used in more or less the same way that we use parsley; a decorative, flavouring garnish. The seeds are strangely flavoured, and are again an essential ingredient of most masalas. They are available whole or ground, and their fragrance is enhanced by a gentle heating in the frying pan before use.

Coriander is quite easy to grow in a sunny window box. Scatter the seeds and water well until germination — about 18 days. Pick the leaves when the plants reach about 6 inches high.

CUMMIN: The seed of a plant of the parsley family, cummin is another important ingredient of most masalas with a powerful, sweet flavour. It is also used in perfumery, and for medicinal purposes.

FENNEL: Closely related to cummin, fennel is available in seed form, or ground. The plant grows happily in most parts of the United Kingdom, and the spiky leaves will give a delicate flavour to salad dishes. There is a Greek myth that knowledge came to man from Olympus in the form of a fiery coal contained in a fennel stalk.

FENUGREEK: This plant has slightly bitter, fragrant seeds which add an interesting flavour to fish and sea food dishes when used sparingly. The green leaves are also used, and both the leaves and seeds are rich in iron.

GINGER: A rhizome with a pungent, yet sweet flavour, ginger should, if possible, be bought in its fresh, root, or 'green' form, as the powder imparts quite a different flavour. Try preserving pieces of root ginger in an airtight jar by covering them with dry sherry.

MINT: The fresh leaves are used as a garnish in Indian cooking, and when chopped the herb makes a pleasant refreshing addition to ratias and chutneys. If using dried mint, substitute half the quantity required for fresh.

MUSTARD SEED: The small reddish brown to black seeds of a type of mustard plant. Mustard oil is used in cooking, particularly in Bengal and Northern India, (and regularly in the Shish Mahal!)

PAPRIKA: The powder made from dried paprika peppers should be mild, sweet, and brilliantly red. It may be used to provide the distinctive red colour in certain Asian foods, as an alternative to large quantites of red chillies.

TAMARIND: The pulp which surrounds the seeds of the Tamarind Tree is dried and sold in packet form in this country.

For use in a recipe, soak a tablespoonfull of the dried pulp in ¼ pint of hot water for 5 - 10 minutes, mixing it in well. Strain out the seeds and fibres. It is preferable to vinegar or lemon juice where sharpness is required.

TURMERIC: A rhizome of the ginger family, turmeric is used ground to impart a yellow colour to food. It has a strong bitter flavour, and should be used sparingly.

GARAM MASALA

Garam masala is a mixture of spices which have been roasted whole, and then ground together to a powder. The type and quantity of spices used varies from region to region, from cook to cook, even from time to time, as you will find yourself. It is this mixture which makes curries so diverse, giving each dish an individuality of its own.

The roasting of the spices not only brings out the flavour, but makes them easier to grind. Use a blender, liquidiser, coffee mill, or mortar and pestle — or if you have none of these, place the spices in a strong brown paper bag, and roll them with a rolling pin until crushed.

There are no 'hot' spices in Ali's garam masala, so you can control the strength of each dish that you make by the number of fresh chillies, or teaspoons of chilli powder that you feel necessary to your taste.

THE SHISH SPICES
coriander seed . . . . 4 tablespoons
white cummin seed . . . . 2½ tablespoons
Stick cinnamon . . . . 4 inches
black cardamom seed . . . . . . 2 teaspoons

Place the coriander seed in a dry frying pan, and roast over a moderately high heat until the aroma wafts up to you. Don't walk away from it, because it will begin to burn as soon as you do! Tip the roasted seeds into your grinding device, then roast the other items individually in the same way. When they are all done, grind them together to a powder. That's it! Keep the masala in an airtight jar, and use generously.

HOME COOKING

SOME USEFUL INFORMATION

The recipes in this book are designed to provide sufficient for at least four servings as a main course with a rice dish.

They will provide up to eight smaller portions when served with a variety of dishes — for example as part of a buffet.

The following menus are suggested as a guide only — the choice of dishes must rest on you, and your guests', personal taste.

SUGGESTED MENU FOR 6:

Starter:	Shami Kebab
Main Course:	Prawn Burryani with Kofta Sauce
	Chicken Dhansak
	Lamb Madras
Accompaniments:	Chapatis
	Special Onion Salad
	Spiced Onion
	Ratia
Dessert:	Kheer (double quantity)

SUGGESTED MENU FOR 8:

Starter:	Vegetable Pakora, Papadams
Main Course:	Tandoori Chicken
	Lamb Quorma
	Scampi Patia
	Bombay Potato
	Pulao Rice
Accompaniments:	Nan Bread
	Mint & Yoghurt Chutney
	Spiced Onion
Dessert:	Gulab Jamin (double quantity)

SUGGESTED VEGETARIAN MENU FOR 6:

Starter:	Pakora, Papadum
Main Course:	Mushroom Burryani with Kofta Sauce
	Indian Vegetable
	Tarka Daal
	Methi Aloo
Accompaniments:	Paratha
	Special Onion Salad
	Mango Chutney
Dessert:	Fernai (double quantity)

WEIGHTS AND MEASUREMENTS — A Guide

Throughout the recipes, imperial weights and their approximate metric equivalents have been given. These are intended as a guide only, as so much depends on individual taste.

The teaspoon referred to is the standard 5ml, the tablespoon 17.7ml, and all spoon measurements are level spoonfulls.

EQUIPMENT

No special Asian cooking utensils are required to prepare these recipes. The following is a list of suitable utensils:

Two or three saucepans of varying sizes, with close fittings lids.

Sharp kitchen knife, and chopping board.

Grinding apparatus: i.e. electric grinder, liquidiser or blender, or a mortar and pestle.

ONIONS — FOR BEGINNERS

To slice an onion, halve it lengthways — i.e. through the root; (1) place each half flat on the chopping board and slice it across with a very sharp knife, beginning at the root end (2). Try to keep the slices in position as you go, retaining the shape of the onion half.

To chop an onion, slice as above (1 & 2), then turn it and slice across at right angles to the first slices (3).

15

To chop an onion finely, halve it as before (1), but this time slice it lengthwise, i.e. from top to root (4). Keeping the slices in position, and watching your fingers very carefully, slice it in half horizontally (5); then slice it across as finely as possible (6).

Should all this bring tears to your eyes, wipe them with a damp cloth for instant relief!

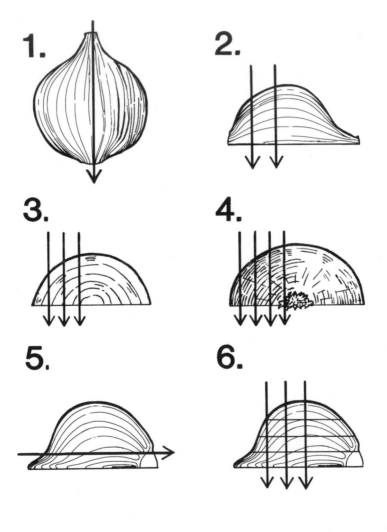

GARLIC AND GINGER

Crushing garlic releases the essential oil and gives more flavour than merely chopping it.

Added to a dish at the end of the cooking time, the smell of crushed garlic will permeate your kitchen, and stay on your breath for hours. However, if you add it towards the beginning of your preparations, it will lose most of its pungency as it cooks slowly and blends harmoniously with the other spices and flavourings.

To prepare garlic cloves for any of Ali's recipes, peel each clove and cut off the root end. If you have a garlic crusher, carry on from there. If not, place the clove on a chopping board, take a broad bladed (cook's) knife, place the blade over the clove and smack it down smartly with the heel of your hand. The clove will be crushed to a pulp, and can now be finely chopped.

Fresh, or root ginger, responds well to the same treatment. Scrape the piece of ginger required, slice it about 1/8" thick. Place the slices flat on the chopping board and crush with the knife and hand, as above. It is much easier to chop in its crushed form.

BONING A CHICKEN

There are several methods of removing chicken meat from the bones. You can joint the chicken, as described under Chicken Tandoori, then scrape the meat from the bones individually. Or you can cut away the meat from the carcass which ever way you please. You will end up with a certain amount of boneless meat, and a certain amount of meat still stuck to the bones. These bones will, of course, make the most marvellous stock, but I prefer to use all the meat in the dish I happen to be preparing, and to put up with a more economical stock made from bones and vegetables.

The simplest way of boning a chicken is to do it all in one, removing the meat from the carcass first, then the limbs. If you follow the instructions you will end up with a whole chicken, without the bones, which you can then stuff with your favourite sage and onion, and reshape into a chicken shape; or you can roll it up and tie it into a sausage or galantine; or you can cut the meat into even-sized pieces, as required for Chicken Tikka.

The only equipment you need is a very sharp knife and a sense of adventure.

1. Take a 3 - 3½lb (approx. 1½ kg) bird. Remove the wings at the second joint, and the last joint of the legs.

2. Place the bird on the chopping board upside down — that is with the backbone facing you. Cut down the line of the backbone from neck to parsons nose, exposing the meat.

3. With the tip of the knife, ease the meat away from the bone, round one side of the body, till you reach the place where the leg joins it. Holding the leg with one hand, and the knife with the other, move the leg about until you can reach the joint with the knife. Cut the ligament at the joint.

    Treat the wing joint in the same way.

4. Now continue cutting the meat away from the body, or carcass, until you reach the breast bone. Do not cut through the skin.

5. Turn the bird round so that the other end is towards you, and the backbone still facing you, and repeat stages 3 and 4 down the other side of the body, till you reach the breast bone.

    Ease the meat gently away from the breast bone without breaking the skin.

6. If you wish to cook the chicken whole, you may prefer to leave the leg and wing bones in position.

    To remove them, cut the skin away from the lower end of the limbs, then using your very sharp knife ease the meat away from the bones, starting from the top, or inside end.

To reshape the chicken, place your stuffing in the centre, sew up the backbone, and truss it quite tightly.

Use the bones with the giblets to make stock, and don't be disappointed if you don't make a neat job of your first boning attempt. The second time you will have a much clearer picture of what is required.

GHEE

This is clarified butter, or pure butter fat. It is fairly easy to make at home, and more economical in the long run than cooking with butter, as it will heat to a much higher temperature and therefore does not burn as readily as butter.

Heat some butter in a heavy based saucepan, until it froths. Skim the froth from the top, allow to cool slightly, then pour off the melted butter fat into another container, leaving the milk solids behind.

Heat the fat again, then strain carefully to remove any remaining solids.

Ghee will keep for several months without refrigeration. 1lb (450g) butter will render about 12oz (375g) ghee.

DRINKS TO ACCOMPANY MEALS

This is very much a matter of personal taste, although strongly-flavoured drinks are not recommended as an accompaniment to heavily spiced foods.

LASSI

A cool refreshing drink to accompany curries, Lassi can be sweetened or salted according to taste.

To make 2 glasses:
natural yoghurt .... 1 tumbler full
milk .... ¾ of a tumbler full
water .... ¼ tumbler full
salt or sugar .... to taste

Blend all the ingredients together in a tall jug, or a blender. Pour into glasses, and add a couple of ice cubes.

An alternative which you may like to try is buttermilk. This is the drink Ali himself prefers, as a natural complement to his dishes.

GLOSSARY

Punjabi	English
Bhoona or Bhujia ..	Meat or vegetable dish with no gravy. (Roasted, Curried)
Burryani	A superior form of pulau
Chapati (Roti) Phulka, Parshada) ..	Simple Indian Bread made from whole wheat flour
Dahl	Indian dried beans and peas commonly called lentils
— Channa dahl	Gram split peas
Dhansak	Meat curry with lentil and Vegetable
Garam Masala	Mixed spices
Ghee	Clarified butter
Gulab Jamin	A fritter soaked in syrup
Kebab	Meat burgers
Kheer	Rice pudding
Kofta	Vegetable or meat balls
Nan	Rich leavened bread
Nargisi Kofta	Egg stuffed meat ball
Pakora	Fritters or scallops
Paratha	An Indian bread, layered/stuffed
Pulau	Fried rice with butter and stuffings
Quorma	Meat curry with yoghurt
Raita	A yoghurt based dish
Shami Kebab	Round meat burgers
Seekh Kebab	Long meat burgers
Tandoor	An Oven
Tikka	Small piece of barbecued meat
Vindaloo	Vinegared meat curry

1

PAKORA

VEGETABLE PAKORA

PAKORA SAUCE

SHAMI KEBAB

PAKORA

The European tradition of serving a "Starter" before the main meal is not customary in Indian or Pakistani households. The Pakora is considered a snack, something to tide you over till dinner time. You can buy them in the streets from traders who will fry them freshly for you, rather as we would expect to buy a hot dog, or hamburger in this country; but there the similarity ends.

Pakoras come in an infinite number of varieties, made with every kind of vegetable imaginable — potatoes, aubergines, cauliflower florets — even green chillies.

Ali has had many requests for his Pakora recipe over the years. The popularity of this simple dish has been prodigious, and it is now Ali's pleasure to share the secret of its success.

PAKORA (makes approximately 24)

Gram flour	1lb/450g
onion	4oz/125g, chopped
salt	1½ teaspoons (to taste)
chilli powder	1 teaspoon
whole coriander seeds	1 teaspoon
whole cummin seeds	1 teaspoon
dried fenugreek leaves (methi)	1 tablespoon, chopped
water	¾ pint
cooking oil	sufficient quantity for deep frying

Sift the flour with the salt and chilli powder, add the chopped onions and methi, the coriander, and cummin and mix together. Make a well in the centre of the mixture and pour in the water. Stir thoroughly till you have a soft dough — use a wooden spoon or your hands, the latter being quicker and more efficient!

Leave the dough to rest for at least 15 minutes.

Heat the oil to about 350°F. A cube of day-old bread should take about 25 seconds to turn golden brown at this temperature.

Take a tablespoon of the mixture and drop it gently into the hot oil. Turn it frequently so that it browns evenly. Once it is coloured uniformly all over, remove from the oil with a slotted spoon, and drain the pakora on kitchen paper.

Repeat the process until the mixture is completely used up.

Fenugreek is available in most supermarkets in seed form, but for this dish Ali uses the leaves of the plant, which he describes as a little like highly flavoured spinach. Most Eastern grocers will supply dried fenugreek leaves.

– – ▬ – –

VEGETABLE PAKORA

Gram flour	1lb/450g
water	¾ pint/475ml
salt	1 teaspoon (to taste)
chilli powder	1 teaspoon
whole coriander seeds	1 teaspoon
whole cummin seeds	1 teaspoon
vegetables (onion, cauliflower, potato)	½lb/225g
cooking oil	sufficient quanitiy for deep frying

To prepare the vegetables, separate the cauliflower into small florets and place in boiling, salted water with a bay leaf, for one minute. Drain and rinse under cold water. Boil the potatoes, drain them, remove the skins while still warm. When they have cooled, cut them into small dice. Peel the onion, and chop finely.

Now follow the directions for Pakora, mixing the prepared vegetables into the flour before adding the water.

PAKORA SAUCE

tomato sauce	8 tablespoons
onion	2 tablespoons, finely chopped
fresh tomatoes	2 tablespoons, finely chopped
chilli powder	½ teaspoon
salt	½ teaspoon
sugar	pinch
green chilli	1 finely chopped (to taste)
water	4 tablespoons

Mix all the ingredients together, at least an hour before serving.

— — — — —

SHAMI KEBAB

minced lamb	1lb/450g
fresh coriander leaves	1 tablespoon, chopped
green chillies	3 chopped
chilli powder	1½ teaspoon
salt	1½ teaspoons, (to taste)
whole cummin seed	1 teaspoon
whole coriander seed	1 teaspoon
cooking oil	sufficient for shallow frying

Mix all the spices with the mince. Divide the mixture into four or five hamburgers, and fry in hot oil or fat until cooked.

Note: If fresh coriander leaves are not available, substitute 2 teaspoons chopped fresh parsley.

RICE DISHES

BOILED RICE

PULAO RICE

LAMB BURRYANI

MUSHROOM BURRYANI

PRAWN BURRYANI

BOILED RICE

In India and Pakistan, long thin grains of rice are preferred – and the better the quality of the rice, the better the result.

Basmati Rice is more expensive than ordinary long grain rice, but it is worth every penny.

If you don't already have a favourite method of boiling rice, try this one.

Measure the rice into a cup. Any cup. A tea cup holds approximately 6oz/185g rice, so use two cups of rice to serve four people. Rinse the rice several times in cold water, and drain.

Take twice the amount of water as rice. In other words, 2 cups of water to 1 cup of rice. Place the rice with the measured water into a large saucepan, with 1-2 teaspoons salt. Cover, and bring to the boil.

As soon as the water boils, turn the heat down as low as you can, leave the lid slightly off the pan to let some steam escape, and simmer gently until the liquid has been absorbed, or until the rice is just cooked – what the Italians call Al Dente.

Don't be feart to take the lid off after 10 - 15 minutes to have a test bite of a grain or two – but mind you don't burn your tongue.

If the water has all been absorbed before the rice is ready, add a small amount of boiling water and stir it through quickly. Replace the lid and continue simmering.

If you have water left in the pan, but the rice is cooked, drain it away.

If you find you have left the rice too long and it seems gooey, all is not lost – place the rice in a sieve or collander and rinse it under hot water. You will need to salt it again, but at least it will be edible – and attractive to look at – if your guests are late!

For fitness conscious people, a simpler method for boiled rice with reduced starch content would be to boil 1 cup of long grain rice (preferably 'Basmati') in 5 to 6 cups of water to which 1½ teaspoons of salt may be added. Keep an eye on it, and boil till the rice is about half cooked. To test, take a couple of grains from the pot and crush them between your thumb and first finger. It is half cooked if you are left with two or three tiny bits of uncooked rice in each grain. At this point take the pot off the hot plate and drain the water leaving only a trace of water in the rice. Put the pot back on a very low heat with the lid tightly in place. Spread about one teaspoonful of margerine on the top of the rice to help maintain its shape and keep the grains separate from each other. In five minutes' time, the rice should be ready to serve.

— — ◼ ◼ —

PULAO RICE

Pulao rice is quite a different kettle of fish, as the saying goes. For one thing, it is cooked in stock with spices, so rinsing it at the end would quite defeat the purpose. However, commonsense will still prevail as long as you remember the rule about never leaving the kitchen.

Make up your own stock if you possibly can.

STOCK
Chicken carcass, and/or Lamb bones
1 onion, stuck with 6 cloves
1 bay leaf
3 black cardamom pods
6 peppercorns
1½ teaspoon salt
water to cover

Place all the ingredients in a large saucepan, cover with water, bring to the boil and simmer as slowly as possible for as long as possible — 3 hours would be lovely.

If you can't make your own stock, dissolve 4 or 5 stock cubes in two pints of water, add the spices from the above list, and simmer for at least 20 minutes. Strain.

PULAO RICE

Long grain (or Basmati) rice ...	1lb/450g
onion	4oz/125g finely chopped
garlic	2 cloves, crushed and finely chopped
fresh ginger	2 teaspoons, finely chopped
tomatoes	2 or 3, 4oz/125g skinned and roughly chopped
turmeric	1 teaspoon
black cardamom (ground)	½ teaspoon
garam masala	1 teaspoon
ghee	4oz/125g
stock (hot)	2 pints/1100 ml

Fry the onion, garlic, ginger and tomatoes in the ghee until soft and golden brown. Add the spices, cook over a gentle heat, and stir well to prevent sticking.

Now add the rice, and continue cooking for several minutes, stirring continuously, until the grains of rice are well coated with the spice mixture.

Remove from the heat, and pour in the warmed stock. Stir through, then cover tightly and simmer over a very low heat for 20 minutes.

When the rice is cooked, remove the cover, fluff the rice up gently with a fork or slotted spoon, and leave for 5 minutes before serving.

— — — —

LAMB BURRYANI

Lamb (leg, fillet or loin)	1lb/450g, boned, trimmed and cubed
water	2½ pints/1½ litres
cinnamon	1" piece of stick
black cardamom pods	5
salt	1½ teaspoons
ghee or butter	4oz/125g
onion	8oz/250g, chopped

garlic	6 cloves, crushed and finely chopped
ginger (fresh)	1oz/30g bruised and finely chopped
tomatoes	4oz/125g skinned and chopped
yoghurt	2 tablespoons
peppercorns	6
cloves	6
turmeric	1 teaspoon
garam masala	2 teaspoons
salt	1 teaspoon
whole cummin seed	1 teaspoon
whole coriander seed	1 teaspoon
long grain (or Basmati) rice . . .	12oz/375g (2 teacups), washed and drained

Place the meat in a large saucepan with the bones, trimmings, water, 1½ teaspoons salt, cinnamon stick and 5 cardamom pods. Bring the water gently to the boil, then remove the meat with a slotted spoon and keep it warm. Continue to simmer the water until you need it for the rice, by which time it should have become well flavoured by the bones and spices.

Melt the ghee or butter in a large frying pan, or flame proof casserole, fry the onion, garlic, ginger and tomato until the onion is golden brown, (about 10 minutes).

Add the turmeric, peppercorns, cloves and salt. Fry gently for two or three minutes, then stir in the yoghurt.

Add the partially cooked meat, and continue cooking until the meat is almost tender, stirring occasionally. Do take care not to over-cook the meat at this stage, as it still has a good twenty minutes to go in the pan.

Now add the whole cummin and coriander seeds, and the rice, and stir them into the spice and meat mixture. Then pour in the drained stock (in which you heated the meat).

Cover the pan tightly, simmer until the liquid has been absorbed by the rice (about 15 minutes).

Sprinkle the garam masala over the top, fluff the rice up with a fork or slotted spoon, and leave for at least 10 minutes in a warm place before serving.

— — — — —

MUSHROOM BURRYANI

Mushrooms	12oz/375g sliced, sprinkled with 2 teaspoons lemon juice
salt	1 teaspoon
mustard oil and ghee	5 tablespoons
onion	8oz/250g finely chopped
tomatoes	4oz/125g skinned and chopped
garlic	3 cloves, crushed and finely chopped
ginger	2 teaspoons, finely chopped
freshly ground black pepper . . .	to taste
cloves	6
turmeric	1 teaspoon
garam masala	1 teaspoon
whole coriander seeds	3 teaspoons
cardamom pods (black)	2 crushed
long grain, or basmati rice	12oz/375g (2 teacups), washed and drained
stock (see Pulao Rice)	2 pints/1100ml warmed

Heat 4 tablespoons of the mustard oil, or ghee and fry the mushrooms gently, turning constantly. They will absorb the oil at first, but as they cook through the oil will 'return'; as soon as this happens, remove the mushrooms, draining the oil back into the pan. Keep the mushrooms warm.

Add the other tablespoon of oil or ghee to the pan. Tip in the onion, tomato, garlic and ginger, 1 teaspoon salt and the pepper, and cook until the onion is soft and golden brown. Then add the cloves, turmeric, coriander seeds and cardamom pods, and continue to cook over a gentle heat for several minutes, stirring constantly.

Mix in the yoghurt, then add the rice and fry for 3 or 4 minutes, stirring well. Remove the pan from the heat, and pour in the stock.

Stir well, to make sure neither the rice nor the spices stick to the bottom of the pan, cover, and simmer until the rice is half cooked — about 10 minutes. Tip the mushrooms over the top of the rice, replace the cover, and continue cooking until the liquid has been absorbed.

Sprinkle the garam masala over, stir through with a fork or slotted spoon — this will distribute the mushrooms and masala throughout the burryani — then place it in a moderate oven (325°F, 160°C, or Gas mark 3) for 10 minutes before serving.

— — — — —

PRAWN BURRYANI

prawns	1lb/450g peeled
lemon juice	2 tablespoons
mustard oil or ghee	4 tablespoons
onion	4oz/125g finely chopped
garlic	3 cloves, crushed and finely chopped
ginger	2 teaspoons, bruised and finely chopped
salt	1½ teaspoons
ground coriander	1 teaspoon
fenugreek seeds	1 teaspoon
turmeric	1 teaspoon
peppercorns	6
cloves	6
black cardamom seeds	½ teaspoon, crushed
tomatoes	6oz/185g skinned and chopped
long grain (Basmati) rice	12oz/385g washed and drained
stock (see Pulao Rice)	scant 2 pints/1100ml warmed
garam masala	2 teaspoons
black cummin seeds	1 teaspoon
fresh coriander leaves	1 tablespoon chopped
lemon and cucumber slices for garnish	

Wash the prawns and dry carefully with kitchen paper. Sprinkle with the lemon juice and leave for 10 minutes.

Heat the oil and fry the onion, garlic, ginger and salt until golden brown. Add the tomatoes and all the spices except for the garam masala and black cummin seeds, fry gently for several minutes, stirring occasionally.

Add the prawns, and one or two tablespoons of the stock, cover, and cook very gently for about seven minutes. The prawns should now be plump and pink. Add the rice, cook and stir until the rice is well mixed in, then add the black cummin seeds and the stock.

Cover, and simmer gently for about 20 minutes, until the liquid has been absorbed by the rice, and the rice is cooked through.

Sprinkle the garam masala, and the chopped coriander leaves, and any lemon juice which may be left from the prawns. Fluff up the rice with a fork, or slotted spoon (which is less likely to break the grains than a wooden spoon), place the burryani in a moderate oven (325°F, 160°C, or Gas Mark 3) for 10 minutes.

Garnish, if you like, with lemon and cucumber slices, sliced hard-boiled egg, and serve on its own, or with a sauce such as the Kofta Curry Sauce.

~ 3 ~
TANDOORI DISHES

TANDOORI CHICKEN

LAMB TIKKA

CHICKEN TIKKA

TURKISH KEBAB

TANDOORI SPECIALITIES

Tandoori food takes its name from the type of oven in which it is cooked — the Tandoor. This is a clay oven, open at the top, with burning coals placed inside in the bottom. The inside is roughly spherical in shape.

The Shish Mahal has two of these ovens, which require a great deal of skill and experience to use. The nature of the Tandoor contributes largely to the flavour of the food cooked in it, and it is virtually impossible to reproduce this effect in the home, but you can approach it very nearly either by using a charcoal fired barbeque, or by cooking under a very hot grill, and turning the food frequently.

TANDOORI CHICKEN

chicken	4 portions, or 1 x 3lb/1½kg chicken
vinegar	¼ pint/150ml
salt	2 tablespoons

MARINADE

red chilli powder	2 teaspoons
garlic	3 cloves
fresh ginger	1 teaspoon
fenugreek leaves (dried)	1 teaspoon
mint	1 teaspoon (dried)
garam masala	2 teaspoons
mustard oil	1 tablespoon
cummin seed	½ teaspoon
red food colouring	2 teaspoons
yoghurt	8 fl oz/200ml

Split the chicken, using either a sharp knife or strong kitchen scissors. Start down the breast bone, and don't be afraid of cutting through bone — it is really quite soft, and cuts easily.

When you have cut through one side, open the chicken out flat, and turn it over, so that the back bone is facing you. Now you can cut along the backbone.

With the chicken in two halves you can see clearly where the leg and breast portions would separate, should you wish to divide the bird into four portions. Trim the end sections of the wings and legs, and use them with the giblets for stock. (See Pulao Rice)

Now, remove the skin from the chicken. It will lift off easily for the most part, needing a little assistance with the knife where it sticks.

Prick the meat thoroughly, sprinkle the vinegar over, and rub in the salt. Leave it for about an hour. Then drain.

In the meantime, prepare the marinade. If you have a blender, or liquidiser, this makes life easier, otherwise it's back to the mortar and pestle. Whichever method you use, crush the garlic and the ginger, place them with the other ingredients in the blender, or mortar, and grind as smoothly as possible.

Coat the drained chicken pieces well with the marinade, cover, and leave for 24 hours.

Place the chicken under a hot grill (or over a hot barbeque!) with as much marinade clinging to it as possible. Cook for about 30 minutes, turning frequently to prevent burning.

Serve Tandoori Chicken with Pulao Rice, salad, generous slices of lemon, and Nan bread.

LAMB TIKKA

leg of Lamb, boned	2lb/900g trimmed and cut into bite-sized pieces
vinegar	3 tablespoons
salt	2 teaspoons

MARINADE

garlic	3 cloves
fresh ginger	1 teaspoon
mint	½ teaspoon dried, 1 teaspoon fresh chopped
garam masala	2 teaspoons
mustard oil	1 tablespoon
turmeric	1 teaspoon
cummin seed (white)	2 teaspoons
red chilli powder	2 teaspoons
yoghurt	3 tablespoons

Sprinkle two tablespoons of the vinegar over the meat, add the salt, and leave while you prepare the marinade.

Crush, and chop finely the garlic and ginger. Mix them with the rest of the vinegar, and the other ingredients. If you are using a blender, or liquidiser, stop the machine occasionally to scrape down the sides. When the mixture is fairly smooth, add it to the meat, and mix well to coat the meat thoroughly. Cover, and leave for 18 to 24 hours.

To cook the tikka, thread the pieces onto skewers, and place under a hot grill, turning frequently, for about 10 minutes.

CHICKEN TIKKA

chicken	approx. 1lb/450g or 1 x 3lb (1½kg) chicken, boned (See Home Cooking)
vinegar	¼ pint/150ml
salt	1 tablespoon

MARINADE

red chilli powder	2 teaspoons
garlic	3 cloves, crushed and chopped finely
fresh ginger	1 teaspoon, bruised and chopped finely
fenugreek leaves (dried)	1 teaspoon
mint	1 teaspoon dried, or 2 teaspoons fresh
garam masala	2 teaspoons
mustard oil	1 tablespoon
cummin seed	½ teaspoon
yoghurt	3 tablespoons

Cut the chicken meat into bite-sized pieces, mix well with the vinegar and salt, and leave for 30 minutes.

Combine the ingredients for the marinade, blend as smoothly as possible, either with a blender or liquidiser, or mortar and pestle.

Drain the chicken well, then mix into the marinade, making sure all the pieces are well coated. Leave for 18 to 24 hours.

Thread the pieces onto skewars and cook under a hot grill for 15 minutes (until the chicken is cooked through), turning frequently.

TURKISH (SEEKH) KEBABS

lamb	1lb/450g minced
garlic	2 cloves, crushed and chopped finely
chilli powder	2 teaspoons
salt	1½ teaspoons
cummin seed (whole)	2 teaspoons
coriander seed (whole)	2 teaspoons
mint or methi	1 teaspoon dried
black pepper	freshly ground, to taste
garam masala	2 teaspoons
mustard oil	2 tablespoons
turmeric	1 teaspoon
green chilli	1-2 chopped
cooking oil	1-2 tablespoons (for basting)

Mix the garlic, and fresh herbs, into the meat, add the spices, and enough mustard oil to bind the mixture together. Leave for several hours before cooking, if possible.

Shape the mixture into sausages about 2" in length, place them lengthways on skewers, and grill under a very hot grill for 10 - 15 minutes, turning frequently, and basting with the oil as necessary.

CHICKEN DISHES

CHICKEN CURRY

CHICKEN WITH BHINDI

CHICKEN VINDALOO

CHICKEN DHANSAK

CHICKEN DO-PIAZZA

BOMBAY CHICKEN

CHICKEN CURRY (1)

chicken	4 portions
onion	8oz/250g sliced
tomatoes	8oz/250g sliced
garlic	3 cloves, crushed and chopped finely
ginger, fresh	1oz/30g bruised and chopped finely
butter	6oz/185g
cardamom pods (black)	2
cloves	3
salt	1½ teaspoons (to taste)
cinnamon	1" piece of stick
turmeric	½ teaspoon
ground cummin seed	2 teaspoons
ground coriander seed	2 teaspoons
chilli powder	2 teaspoons

Fry the onion, fresh tomatoes, ginger, garlic, cloves, cardamom and cinnamon stick in the butter. When the onions are golden brown add the rest of the ingredients. Mix well, and cook over a low heat for about 8 - 10 minutes. Then add the chicken pieces and cook for several minutes, turning once.

Add enough water to form a thick gravy. Cover, and simmer gently until the chicken is cooked through — about 30 minutes. Stir occasionally, and add more water if the sauce becomes too thick.

CHICKEN WITH BHINDI

chicken	4 portions
onion	8oz/250g sliced
tomatoes	4oz/125g sliced
bhindi (lady fingers, or okra)	8oz/250g trimmed and sliced thickly
garlic	3 cloves, crushed and sliced finely
ginger	1oz/30g bruised and chopped finely
ghee or butter	4oz/125g
black cardamom (ground)	½ teaspoon
salt	1½ teaspoons
turmeric	1 teaspoon
chilli powder	2 teaspoons
ground cummin seed	2 teaspoons
ground coriander seed	2 teaspoons
garam masala	2 tablespoons
water	scant ½ pint/300ml

Fry the onion and tomatoes with the garlic, ginger, and spices, but retain the garam masala until the end of the cooking period.

Add the bhindi and the chicken pieces, fry for several minutes, stirring the pan constantly, to avoid sticking. Pour in sufficient water to make a thick sauce, cover, and simmer for 30 to 40 minutes, or until the chicken is cooked, and the bhindi tender.

Sprinkle the garam masala, and leave for 5 minutes before serving with plain or pulao rice.

CHICKEN VINDALOO

Chicken	4 portions
butter or ghee	2 tablespoons
mustard oil	3 tablespoons
onion	8oz/250g sliced
garlic	5 cloves, crushed and finely chopped
ginger	two teaspoons, bruised and finely chopped
cardamom pods (black)	2
fenugreek seeds	1 teaspoon
cloves	8
turmeric	1 teaspoon
cinnamon	1" piece of stick
paprika	1 teaspoon
red chilli powder	2 teaspoons
mustard seed	2 teaspoons
white cummin seed	2 teaspoons
black cummin seed	2 teaspoons
coriander seed	2 teaspoons
tomatoes	8oz/250g sliced or 1 x 15oz/400g can
potatoes	8oz/250g cooked and diced
salt	1½ teaspoons
tamarind water	¼ pint/150ml (see Spices chapter)
fresh green chillies	2 (or more) sliced
garam masala	1 tablespoon

First, place all the whole spices in a dry frying pan, and roast them together over a moderate heat for 8 - 10 minutes. Do not allow them to burn!

If you don't like to crunch whole spices when you eat Chicken Vindaloo, grind the roasted spices to a powder before frying them.

Melt the butter or ghee with the oil, add the onion, garlic, ginger and spices, and fry them gently for several minutes, stirring constantly.

If you are using canned tomatoes, drain them, and reserve the liquid. Add the tomatoes to the frying pan with the chicken pieces, cook for 10 minutes, turning the chicken once or twice.

Now add the salt, tamarind liquid and chopped green chillies and potatoes. If the sauce is too thick, use the reserved liquid from the tomatoes to thin it. Otherwise, add water.

Cover, and simmer gently for 40 - 50 minutes, until the chicken is tender and cooked through. Sprinkle the garam masala over the top and leave for 10 minutes before serving.

Curried dishes seem to gain even more flavour, and power, if left in the deep freeze for a day or more. Why not make up a double recipe, and keep some in hand for a later occasion?

CHICKEN DHANSAK

chicken	4 portions
lentils	8oz/250g washed, steeped in boiling water for 10 mins and drained
ghee or oil	4oz/125g
tomatoes	4oz/125g sliced
garlic	6 cloves, crushed and chopped finely
ginger	1oz/30g bruised and chopped finely
chilli powder	2 teaspoons
fresh green chilli	2 (optional) sliced
salt	1½ teaspoons
cloves	3
black cardamon (ground)	½ teaspoon
cummin (ground)	1 teaspoon
coriander (ground)	1 teaspoon
fenugreek seeds	1 teaspoon
fennel (ground)	1 teaspoon
turmeric	1 teaspoon
mint	2 teaspoons dried, or 1 tablespoon fresh
garam masala	1 tablespoon

Heat the ghee or oil, and fry the sliced onion, tomato, garlic and ginger until soft. Place half the mixture in a large saucepan with the lentils, sliced green chilli, salt, and enough water to cover. Bring to the boil, cover, and simmer gently for 10 minutes or so, until the liquid has been absorbed. Turn into a sieve or blender and puree well.

In the meantime, add the remaining ingredients to the mixture still in the frying pan, with the chicken, and about ¼ pint (150ml) water. Cover, and simmer gently until the meat is cooked. Turn the chicken pieces over once or twice during this period to ensure even cooking.

Add the lentil puree, stir well, check the seasoning, and if the sauce seems very thick, add a little water, or lemon juice.

Turmeric is used as a cosmetic in some parts of the Far East, to impart a golden glow to the skin.

— — — — —

CHICKEN DO-PIAZZA

chicken	4 portions
onions	4oz/125g finely chopped
	12oz/375g finely sliced
garlic	6 cloves, crushed and finely sliced
ginger	1oz/30g bruised and finely chopped
ghee or butter	4oz/125g
mustard oil	1 tablespoon
peppercorns	6
cloves	6
cardamom pods (black)	6 bruised
cinnamon	1" piece of stick
cummin seed	1 teaspoon
coriander seed	2 teaspoons
red chilli powder	2 teaspoons
fennel seeds	½ teaspoon
tomatoes	8oz/250g sliced
salt	1½ teaspoons
garam masala	1 tablespoon
water or stock	½ pint/300ml

We suggest that you prepare the onions for this dish before you do anything else (refer to the chapter on Home Cooking) if for no better reason than the fact that it is the onions which give the recipe its name! Also, you can get the tears over and done with, wipe your eyes with a damp cloth, and then be able to see what you are doing with the rest of the ingredients.

Melt the ghee with the mustard oil and fry the sliced onion, stirring frequently, until it is evenly browned. Remove the onion from the pan, draining the oil back into the pan, and keep warm.

Now fry the finely chopped onion with the garlic, ginger, fennel, peppercorns, cloves, cardamom, cinnamon, cummin, coriander and chilli powder, stirring occasionally, for about 10 minutes.

Add the chicken pieces, fry for about 5 minutes on each side, then add the tomatoes, salt and water or stock.

If you have time to cook this dish very slowly in a warm oven, (e.g. 2 to 3 hours at 300°F, 150°C, or Gas mark 3) then water is perfectly adequate to form the sauce; but if you need to cook it faster, either on the hob or in the oven at 200°C, 400°F, or Gas mark 6, for 40 minutes, then using stock will give the dish a better flavour.

Add the garam masala and the fried onions about 10 minutes before you wish to serve up.

Bombay is India's major western seaport. Built on a group of Islands joined by causeways, the view from the sea shows the city against a backdrop of the Western Ghats mountains.

Apart from being the country's commercial centre, Bombay has a reputation for superb fish and seafood, including Bombay duck. This is not duck at all, but a dried fish which can be fried, cooked in a sauce, or eaten plain. The taste is unbelievably salty, comparable, I should think, to our own Scots salt herring.

BOMBAY CHICKEN

chicken	4 portions
onion	8oz/250g sliced
tomatoes	1lb/450g sliced
garlic	3 cloves, crushed and chopped finely
ginger	1oz/30g bruised and chopped finely
butter or ghee	4oz/125g
cardamom pods (black)	2
cloves	3
salt	1½ teaspoons
fenugreek seeds	½ teaspoon
cinnamon	1" piece of stick
turmeric	½ teaspoon
chilli powder	2 teaspoons
tomato puree	2 teaspoons
fresh chillies	2 sliced (optional)
garam masala	1 tablespoon
eggs	2 hard boiled, sliced

Melt the ghee or butter, and fry the onions, garlic, ginger and half the tomatoes only, with the cardamom, cloves and cinnamon stick. When the onions are soft, and golden brown, add the salt, fenugreek seeds, turmeric, chilli powder and tomato puree. Cook over a low heat for several minutes, stirring constantly.

Now place the chicken pieces in the pan, and turn up the heat slightly. Cook for about 20 minutes, turning the pieces over two or three times.

Stir in enough water to make a thick gravy, cover, and simmer for another 20 minutes.

Remove the cover, sprinkle on the garam masala and the sliced green chillies (if used).

Lastly, add the remaining sliced tomatoes, and the sliced hard boiled eggs, and stir through gently to distribute them evenly. Replace the lid, remove the pan from the heat, and leave for 5/10 minutes before serving.

LAMB DISHES

BHOONA LAMB

BAGON GOSHT

LAMB MADRAS

LAMB QUORMA

MUTTON BANDALOO

LAMB PATIA

LAMB PUNJABI MASALA

DAAL GOSHT

BHOONA LAMB

lamb (leg or fillet)	2lb/900g trimmed and cubed
onion	8oz/250g sliced
garlic	4 cloves, crushed and sliced finely
fresh ginger	1oz/30g bruised and chopped finely
ghee or butter	4oz/125g
black cardamom pods	2
black mustard seed	½ teaspoon
cloves	5
cinnamon	2" piece of stick
cummin seed	1 teaspoon
turmeric	½ teaspoon
chilli powder	2 teaspoons (more if liked)
tomatoes	8oz/250g sliced
tomato puree	1 tablespoon
sugar	½ teaspoon
salt	1½ teaspoons
water	½ pint/150ml
garam masala	2 tablespoons
lemon juice	1 tablespoon

Fry the onion, garlic and ginger in the melted ghee or butter until the onion is soft, and golden brown. Add the cardamom pods, mustard seed, cloves, cinnamon, cummin, turmeric and chilli powder, and cook for at least 10 minutes, stirring frequently.

Now add the meat, tomatoes, tomato puree, sugar and salt. Continue to cook over a moderate heat until the meat is lightly browned.

Add the water, cover, and simmer very slowly until the meat is tender (about 35 minutes), sprinkle the garam masala and lemon juice over, and check the sauce. Bhoona lamb is a dry recipe, so most of the liquid should have disappeared. If, however, the liquid cooks out before the meat is ready, don't hesitate to add a little more hot water as necessary.

BAGON GOSHT (Aubergines)

Lamb (leg or fillet)	1lb/450g trimmed and cubed
aubergines (eggplant)	1lb/450g
onion	4oz/125g sliced
tomatoes	8oz/250g sliced
garlic	3 cloves, crushed and finely chopped
ginger	1oz/30g finely chopped
ghee or butter	4oz/125g
cummin (ground)	2 teaspoons
coriander (ground)	2 teaspoons
cloves	5
cinnamon	2" piece of stick
cardamom pods (black)	3
turmeric	½ teaspoon
chilli powder	2 teaspoons
salt	1½ teaspoons
water	½ pint/300ml
garam masala	1 tablespoon
lemon juice	2 teaspoons

Prepare the aubergines by placing them under a hot grill, about 6" from the element, turning them until the skin is black all over. Allow them to cool slightly, then strip away the skin, and chop the flesh roughly.

Fry the onion, garlic and ginger in the melted ghee, with the tomatoes and chopped aubergines, until the onion is golden brown, and the aubergines soft. Add the ground cummin and coriander, cloves, cinnamon stick, cardamom pods, turmeric, chilli powder and salt.

Fry the spices with the vegetable for 10 minutes, stirring frequently.

Add the lamb, and cook until the meat is sealed on all sides. Remove the pan from the heat, stir in the water. Cover, and return to the heat. Simmer gently for half an hour, or until the meat is cooked.

Sprinkle the garam masala over, with the lemon juice, and keep warm for several minutes before serving.

Ali uses leg of lamb in all his lamb recipes, as this is the prime cut. If you wish to substitute a more economical cut, such as shoulder, an adjustment in the cooking time is required, as explained in the following recipe.

LAMB MADRAS

lamb	2lb/900g trimmed and cubed
onion	8oz/250g sliced
tomatoes	4oz/125g sliced
garlic	3 cloves, crushed and finely chopped
fresh ginger	1oz/30g bruised and finely chopped
cardamom pods (black)	4
cinnamon	2" piece of stick
cloves	5
ghee or butter	4oz/125g
salt	1½ teaspoons
turmeric	½ teaspoon
ground cummin	3 teaspoons
coriander (ground)	3 teaspoons
red chilli powder	3 teaspoons
water	½ pint/300ml
garam masala	2 tablespoons
lemon juice	2 tablespoons
fresh green chillies	2 or more (to taste)

Melt the ghee in a large frying pan, or heat proof casserole, fry the onion, tomatoes, garlic and ginger over a moderate heat until the onion is golden brown.

Add the rest of the spices except for the garam masala and green chillies, and fry gently for about 10 minutes, stirring occasionally to prevent sticking.

Add the meat, and continue to cook over gentle heat, stirring, until the meat is well coated in the spice mixture.

52

If you are not using leg of lamb, patience at this stage will pay dividends. The more slowly you cook the meat, the more the spices will permeate it, breaking down the fibres gradually, giving you tender, yet juicy pieces of lamb or mutton.

Add enough water to form a thin gravy, cover and leave to simmer gently until the meat is tender, 30 - 40 minutes for leg of lamb, 1½ - 2 hours for shoulder, or stewing lamb. Sprinkle the garam masala and lemon juice over, stir in the chopped green chilli, and remember, this is what makes a Madras Curry the delight of fire eaters the world over, so be warned! Leave it to cook for a further 10 - 15 minutes.

— — — —

LAMB QUORMA

lamb	2lb/900g leg or fillet, boned and diced
onion	4oz/125g sliced
garlic	3 cloves, finely sliced
fresh ginger	2 teaspoons, bruised and chopped finely
cardamom pods (black)	3
cloves	5
cinnamon	2" stick
turmeric	½ teaspoon
ground cummin	2 teaspoons
ground coriander	2 teaspoons
red chilli powder	2 teaspoons
garam masala	1 tablespoon
water	½ pint/300ml
yoghurt (plain)	5 fl oz/150ml
salt	1½ teaspoons
coconut (creamed or dessicated)	6oz/185g
tomatoes	4oz/125g chopped finely
fresh coriander leaves	2 tablespoons (optional)

Fry the onion, garlic and ginger, until the onion is soft, add the spices, excluding the garam masala at this stage.

Cook gently but thoroughly for about 20 minutes, stirring the pan occasionally to prevent sticking.

Add the meat, increase the heat to moderate and continue to fry until the meat is well coloured. Pour in the water, cover, and simmer gently until the meat is tender, about 35 minutes.

Now add the tomatoes, salt, garam masala and coconut, and simmer until the sauce has almost evaporated, then add the yoghurt and coriander leaves (if used). Heat through, and serve.

If you prefer a 'hotter' sauce, try adding a few chopped green chillies at the end. On the other hand, if it is too hot, add some more yoghurt, and a squeeze of lemon juice; even another tablespoon or two of coconut will tame it down a little.

Indeed, the real secret of home cooked curries lies in experimentation. Don't be frightened to leave out the garlic if your mother-in-law can't eat it. Your Quorma will be different, but still delicious.

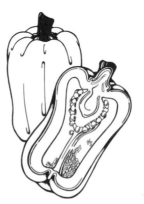

MUTTON BANDALOO

lamb or mutton	1½lb/750g, trimmed and cubed
onion	8oz/250g sliced
tomatoes	4oz/125g sliced
potatoes	1lb/450g peeled and diced
garlic	4 cloves, crushed and finely chopped
ginger	1 teaspoon finely chopped
cloves	4
cardamom pods (black)	3
cinnamon	1" piece of stick
turmeric	1 teaspoon
coriander seeds (whole)	1 teaspoon
red chilli powder	2 teaspoons
tamarind water	¼ pint/150ml
salt	2 teaspoons
water	1 pint/550ml
ghee or cooking oil	4oz/125g
garam masala	1 tablespoon

Heat the ghee or oil and fry the onion and garlic with the whole spices until the onion is soft and golden brown. Add the ground spices and meat, cook until the meat is sealed. (i.e. browned on all sides)

Add the tomatoes, potatoes, water, tamarind water and salt, cover and cook for a further 40 minutes or so, until the meat is tender, and the potatoes cooked.

Stir in the garam masala just before serving.

LAMB PATIA

lamb	2lb/900g trimmed and cubed
onion	8oz/250g sliced
tomatoes	8oz/250g sliced
garlic	3 cloves, crushed and finely chopped
ginger	1oz/30g bruised and finely chopped
ghee or butter	4oz/125g
ground cummin	2 teaspoons
ground coriander	2 teaspoons
cardamom pods (black)	5
cloves	5
peppercorns	5
cinnamon	2" piece of stick
mint	2 teaspoons dried, or 1 tablespoon fresh
tomato puree	1 tablespoon
sugar	½ teaspoon (a pinch)
salt	1½ teaspoons (to taste)
mango chutney	2 heaped tablespoons
dessicated coconut	1 tablespoon
water	½ pint/300ml
garam masala	1 tablespoon

Melt the ghee or butter, fry the onion, tomatoes, garlic and ginger with the salt and spices – reserving the garam masala till the end of the cooking period.

Add the meat and continue cooking over a moderate heat for 10 minutes or so, stirring occasionally. Don't let the mixture stick to the bottom of the pan.

Stir in the tomato puree and sugar with the coconut and water. Cover and cook gently for 30 - 40 minutes, or until the meat is tender.

Lastly, add the mango chutney and garam masala, heat through and serve.

Watchpoint: Don't add mango chutney to the dish unless you are sure you are ready to serve up, as the mango will toughen if left to cook for any length of time.

– – – –

LAMB PUNJABI MASALA

THE MASALA

coriander seeds	2 teaspoons
black cardamom seeds	½ teaspoon
peppercorns	½ teaspoon
dried red chillies	6
cinnamon	2" piece of stick
coconut (dessicated)	1 tablespoon
poppy seed	1 teaspoon
turmeric	½ teaspoon
onion	4oz/125g finely chopped

LAMB PUNJABI

lamb	2lb/900g boned, trimmed and cubed
mustard oil	4 tablespoons
onion	4oz/125g finely sliced
tomatoes	8oz/250g sliced
green peppers (capsicum)	8oz/250g seeded and sliced
garlic	2 cloves, crushed and chopped finely
ginger	1oz/30g chopped finely
tomato puree	2 tablespoons
sugar	pinch
salt	1½ teaspoons
water	scant 1 pint/600ml
garam masala	2 teaspoons
lemon juice	1 tablespoon

First, prepare the special Masala. Roast the coriander, cardamom and poppy seeds, the peppercorns, and the cinnamon. Placing them in a dry frying pan over a high heat, until the seeds start to move about in the pan, should do the trick. Now place all the masala ingredients in a blender, or mortar and pestle, and grind them to a paste.

If you have a temperamental liquidiser, which doesn't like dry pastey mixtures, add a little water until it will work.

Blanch the sliced green peppers in boiling water for one minute, then drain.

Heat the mustard oil in a large pan, fry the 4oz/125g sliced onion with the tomatoes and green peppers, garlic and ginger until the onions and peppers are very soft. Now add the Masala which you have just prepared. Fry it all together over a moderate heat, stirring frequently, for 10 minutes.

Raise the heat a little, add the meat, and cook for several minutes. Try to get the meat nicely browned all over before you add the water, with the tomato puree, sugar and salt.

Now cover the pan, turn the heat down very low, and leave to cook as slowly as possible for 1 - 1½ hours.

Just before serving, stir in the garam masala and lemon juice. Heat through.

Try serving Lamb Punjabi Masala with Pulao rice, and Tarka Dall.

DAAL GOSHT

lamb	2lb/900g leg or fillet trimmed and cubed
onion	4-6oz/125-185g chopped
garlic	4 cloves, crushed and finely chopped
ginger	2 teaspoons finely chopped
butter or ghee	4oz/125g
cloves	6
cardamom pods (black)	3
cummin seeds	1 teaspoon
ground cummin	1 teaspoon
coriander seeds	1 teaspoon
cinnamon	1" piece of stick
turmeric	1 teaspoon
tomatoes	8oz/250g chopped roughly
salt	1½ teaspoons (to taste)
red chilli powder	2 teaspoons
fresh green chillies	1 or 2 seeded and sliced
lentils	8oz/250g soaked for 1 hour and drained
water	1 pint/550ml
garam masala	1 tablespoon

Fry the onion, garlic and ginger in the melted ghee for a few minutes, then add the cloves, cardamom, cummin (seeds and powder), coriander, cinnamon and turmeric. Fry gently, stirring frequently, until the onion is well browned.

Add the meat with the tomatoes, salt and chilli powder, and continue to cook until the tomatoes are very soft.

Now add the lentils, green chillies and water. Stir well, cover, and leave to simmer gently for 40 minutes, or until the lentils have disintegrated into the sauce.

Sprinkle over the garam masala, and leave for 5 minutes before serving. You may need to add a little water (or lemon juice, if you prefer) towards the end of the cooking period.

MINCE DISHES

METHI KEEMA

KOFTA CURRY

MINCE PUNJABI MASALA

METHI KEEMA

minced lamb	1lb/450g
methi (fresh or dry fenugreek leaves)	4 tablespoons, chopped
onion	4oz/125g finely chopped
garlic	2 cloves, crushed and finely chopped
ginger (fresh)	2 teaspoons finely chopped
ghee or butter	3 tablespoons
tomato puree	1 tablespoon
turmeric	1 teaspoon
red chilli powder	2 teaspoon
coriander seeds	1 teaspoon
ground cummin	1 teaspoon
cinnamon	1" piece of stick, crushed with a rolling pin
cloves	3
salt	1½ teaspoons (to taste)
yoghurt	2 tablespoons
garam masala	1 tablespoon
water	¼ pint/150ml

Place the methi in a bowl, and pour boiling water over. Leave for one minute, then drain thoroughly.

Melt the ghee or butter, fry the onion with the garlic and ginger until the onion is golden brown. Add the salt, spices and methi, but retain the garam masala for the moment. Continue cooking over a low heat for 10 minutes or so, stirring frequently.

Tip in the minced lamb, and cook until the meat changes colour, then add the yoghurt, tomato puree and water and mix in thoroughly.

Cover, and cook very slowly for about 30 minutes, checking the pan occasionally to make sure nothing is sticking to the bottom.

Stir in the garam masala just before serving.

Both chillies and fenugreek have been considered valuable aids to digestion over the years.

— — — — —

KOFTA CURRY

MINCE BALLS

minced lamb	1lb/450g
chilli powder	2 teaspoons
salt	1 teaspoon
cummin seed	2 teaspoons
coriander seed	2 teaspoons
onion	4oz/125g very finely chopped (see Home Cooking)
freshly ground black pepper . . .	to taste
egg	1 medium
oil (cooking)	sufficient for deep frying (optional)

SAUCE

ghee or butter	2 tablespoons
onion	4oz/125g sliced
garlic	3 cloves, crushed and finely chopped
ginger	4 teaspoons finely chopped
cloves	5
cardamom pods (black)	4 bruised
ground coriander	2 teaspoons
chilli powder	2 teaspoons
salt	1 teaspoon
tomatoes	1 - 15oz/400g can
tomato puree	1 tablespoon
sugar	pinch
yoghurt	4 tablespoons
garam masala	1 tablespoon

To make the meat balls, mix all the ingredients together thoroughly in a bowl, form into plum-sized balls, and either deep fry in the oil, or roast in a moderately hot oven (400°F, 200°C, Gas mark 6), on a greased baking tray, for 20 minutes. Drain well on absorbent paper.

Make sauce by frying the onion, garlic and ginger until soft and golden brown, add the spices and fry for several minutes longer, stirring continuously. Do not include the garam masala at this stage.

Then add all the other ingredients, and finally, the meat balls. Cover partially, and simmer very gently for 40 minutes, by which time the sauce will have thickened. Check the seasoning. Sprinkle on the garam masala and leave for 5 minutes before serving.

A variation on this dish is NARGISI KOFTA, which is a kind of Asian Scotch egg. Divide the mince mixture into six portions, and wrap each portion round a hard boiled egg. Roll the mince-covered egg in seasoned flour, and deep fry for 4/5 minutes, turning frequently to ensure even cooking. Serve sliced in half, so that the egg is visible, and hand the sauce separately.

— — ▬ — —

MINCE PUNJABI MASALA

Prepare as for Lamb Punjabi Masala, except that the meat is minced finely before being added to the spices.

Lahore is the second largest city in Pakistan, and was the capital of the Punjab for over nine centuries. Many fine buildings remain from the days of the Moghul emperors Jahangir and Shah Jahan, and close by are the famous Shahdara and Shalimar gardens. The old city was originally surrounded by a brick wall and a moat, with thirteen gates leading into the inner region.

Most of this has now gone, replaced by gardens which are a popular feature of Lahore.

FISH DISHES

SCAMPI PATIA

KING PRAWN BHOONA

FISH CURRY MASALA

SCAMPI PATIA (Sweet n' Sour Scampi)

scampi	1lb/450g peeled, washed and dried
lemon juice	2 tablespoons
onion	4oz/125g finely chopped
garlic	2 cloves, crushed and finely chopped
ginger	2 teaspoons, bruised and finely chopped
ghee or butter	4oz/125g
fenugreek seeds	½ teaspoon
ground cardamom (black)	½ teaspoon
cloves	3
cinnamon	½" piece of stick, crushed with a rolling pin
turmeric	½ teaspoon
chilli powder	2 teaspoons
cummin seeds, ground	2 teaspoons
coriander, ground	2 teaspoons
tomatoes	8oz/250g chopped
salt	1½ teaspoons
mango chutney	2 tablespoons
garam masala	1 tablespoon

Sprinkle the lemon juice over the scampi, and leave to marinate for 30 minutes.

Fry the onion, garlic and ginger with the spices until the onion is golden brown. Add the tomatoes, salt and scampi, cover, and simmer gently for 20 minutes, until the scampi is firm and bright pink. Add a little water if necessary.

Then add the mango chutney and garam masala. Heat through, and serve — preferably with plain rice.

KING PRAWN BHOONA

King Prawns	1lb/450g peeled, washed and dried
onion	4oz/125g chopped
garlic	3 cloves, crushed and chopped finely
ginger	2 teaspoons crushed and chopped finely
tomatoes	8oz/250g peeled and chopped
butter	4oz/125g
fenugreek seeds	1 teaspoon
cloves	4
cardamom pods (black)	2
cinnamon	1" stick
turmeric	½ teaspoon
chilli powder	2 teaspoons
salt	1½ teaspoons
tamarind water	¼ pint/150ml
spring onions	2 chopped

Melt the butter, fry the onion, garlic, ginger, tomatoes, fenugreek seeds, cloves, cardamom and cinnamon until the onion is golden brown. Add the salt, turmeric and chilli powder and the prawns, and continue cooking until the prawns are firm, and bright pink. Stir in the tamarind water, cover, and simmer gently for about 10 minutes.

Lastly, stir in the chopped spring onions, and cook for another 5 minutes, with the lid off.

FISH CURRY MASALA

cod or haddock	1lb/450g filleted
onion	8oz/250g half sliced, and half finely chopped
garlic	3 cloves, crushed and finely chopped
ginger	1 teaspoon, bruised and finely chopped
ghee or butter	3 tablespoons
coriander leaves	2 tablespoons, chopped
ground cummin	1 teaspoon
ground turmeric	1 teaspoon
chilli powder	2 teaspoons
cloves	4
cinnamon	1" piece of stick, crushed
fenugreek leaves	1 tablespoon, chopped and blanched in boiling water for 1 minute
fenugreek seeds	½ teaspoon
cardamom (ground)	½ teaspoon
water	½ pint/300ml
salt	1½ teaspoons

Prepare the Masala by combining the chopped onion with the garlic, ginger, coriander leaves, cummin, turmeric, chilli powder, cardamom and fenugreek.

Melt the ghee, fry the sliced onion with the cloves and salt until the onion is golden brown. Add the prepared masala and fry gently, stirring constantly, for several minutes.

Stir in the water, and bring to the boil. Add the fish, and turn down the heat to very low. Cover, and simmer gently for 10 minutes.

If the sauce is too thin, add a teaspoon or two of tomato puree, and remember to check the seasoning.

8
VEGETABLE CURRIES

EGG BANDALOO

VEGETABLE CURRY

INDIAN VEGETABLE

TARKA DAAL

BOMBAY POTATO

METHI ALOO

EGG BANDALOO

potatoes	1lb/450g peeled and diced
eggs	4 hard boiled for 10 minutes, shelled
ghee or butter	2 tablespoons
onion	4oz/125g finely chopped
ground cummin	2 teaspoons
ground coriander	2 teaspoons
turmeric	½ teaspoon
fresh green chilli	1 seeded and sliced
water	½ pint/300ml
tomato puree	1 tablespoon
sugar	pinch
garam masala	2 teaspoons

You may like to prepare this dish with small new potatoes, in which case just scrape them, ready for cooking.

Melt the ghee and toss in the onion, garlic, cummin, coriander, turmeric and chilli.

When the onions are soft and well browned, add the potatoes, and coat them well with the spices. Then add the water, and salt to taste, tomato puree, sugar and eggs.

Cover tightly, and cook gently until the potatoes are cooked, about 15 minutes.

Sprinkle the garam masala over, cover and leave a further 5 minutes, then stir through and serve.

You may prefer to slice the eggs just before serving, rather than leaving them whole.

VEGETABLE CURRY

Potatoes	6oz/185g peeled and diced
cauliflower	6oz/185g
peas	4oz/125g
onion	4oz/125g sliced
garlic	2 cloves, crushed and finely chopped
ginger	1oz/30g bruised and finely chopped
tomatoes	4oz/125g chopped
turmeric	1 teaspoon
chilli powder	1½ teaspoons
water	¾ pint/450ml
garam masala	2 teaspoons
ghee or butter	4 tablespoons

Melt the ghee or butter, and fry the onion, garlic and ginger until golden brown. Add the tomatoes, turmeric, chilli powder and salt, and cook for 5 more minutes.

Divide the cauliflower into florets and add them, with the potatoes, to the spice mixture in the pan. Coat them well, and then pour in the water. Cover, and simmer gently for 10 minutes, then add the peas and cook for a further 8-10 minutes.

Sprinkle the garam masala over, leave for 5 minutes before serving.

INDIAN VEGETABLE

Bhindi (Lady fingers of Orka)	5oz/156g trimmed and sliced
aubergine (eggplant)	5oz/156g peeled and sliced
tinda (squash)	3oz/94g diced
karela (bitter gourd)	5oz/156g peeled and diced
cooking salt	2 tablespoons
onion	4oz/125g finely chopped
garlic	2 cloves, crushed and finely chopped
ginger	2 teaspoons grated or finely chopped
turmeric	1 teaspoon
chilli powder	1 teaspoon
salt	1½ teaspoons
garam masala	1 - 2 tablespoons
water	½ pint/300ml
ghee or cooking oil	4 tablespoons

Keeping the aubergine and karela separate, sprinkle them both thickly with the cooking salt, and leave for several hours if possible. Then drain away the water which will have collected, and rinse them well. The karela will now need to be blanched in boiling water for two minutes.

Melt the ghee, and fry the onion, garlic, ginger, with the turmeric, chilli powder and salt, until the onion is well cooked and golden brown. Add all the vegetables, and fry gently for 10 minutes or so.

Add the water, cover and cook for a further 10 minutes, until the vegetables are tender. Sprinkle the garam masala over. If the sauce is too thin, boil it away quickly for a minute.

TARKA DAAL

lentils	8oz/250g rinsed and drained
water	1½ pints/850ml
onion	8oz/250g chopped finely
chilli powder	1 teaspoon
butter or ghee	2oz/60g
garlic	2 cloves, crushed and chopped finely
ginger	1 tablespoon, bruised and chopped finely
salt	1 teaspoon (to taste)
green chilli	1 or 2 sliced (optional)

Place the lentils in a large saucepan with the water, the chilli powder, salt, and half the chopped onion. Bring to the boil.

In the meantime, fry the remaining onion with the garlic and ginger, and the green chilli (if used), in the butter until golden brown. Add this mixture to the lentils, stir through, and continue to cook slowly until the lentils are soft.

If necessary, add more water, or, if there is too much liquid, raise the heat and boil it away — but watch for the lentils sticking to the bottom of the pan. It's better to cook them gently, but thoroughly.

This makes a delicious supper on its own, or it is a perfect accompaniment to a Vindaloo.

— — — —

BOMBAY POTATO

potatoes	1lb/450g peeled and diced
onions	1lb/450g sliced
garlic	2 cloves, crushed and chopped finely
ginger	2oz/56g crushed and chopped finely

tomatoes	8oz/250g chopped roughly
ghee or butter	4oz/125g
salt	1½ teaspoons
chilli powder	2 teaspoons
turmeric	1 teaspoon
garam masala	2 teaspoons
water	¾ pint/450ml

Melt the ghee or butter in a large saucepan. Fry the onions with the garlic and ginger until they are golden brown. Add the tomatoes, salt, chilli powder and turmeric, and cook for 5 minutes.

Add the diced potatoes, stir well, then add the water. Cover the pan, and simmer gently until the potatoes are cooked. Sprinkle over the garam masala, and check the sauce, which should be quite thick.

– – – –

METHI ALOO

potatoes	1lb/450g boiled and diced
methi (fenugreek leaves)	8oz/250g chopped
onion	8oz/250g sliced
ghee or butter	1 tablespoon
garlic	1 clove, crushed and chopped finely
ginger	1 teaspoon chopped finely
salt	½ teaspoon
chilli powder	½ teaspoon

Drop the methi into boiling water for 1 minute. Drain. Fry the onion, garlic and ginger in the melted ghee with the salt.

When the onion is golden brown, add the chilli powder and methi. Cook for several minutes, stirring continuously, then add the diced potatoes.

Reduce the heat, and toss gently together until the potato is heated through, and well coated with the spices.

9
CHILDREN'S DISHES

LAMB CURRY

CHICKEN CURRY

CHILDREN'S LASSI

LAMB CURRY

leg of lamb, boned	2lb/900g trimmed and cut into bite-sized pieces
onion	4oz/125g finely chopped
garlic	4 cloves, crushed and finely chopped
fresh ginger	2 teaspoons grated or finely chopped
cinnamon	1" piece of stick
cloves	6
cardamom pods (black)	6 bruised
ground cummin	2 teaspoons
ghee or butter	4 tablespoons
salt	2 teaspoons
mint, or coriander leaves	1 tablespoon chopped
yoghurt	8 fl oz/220ml
red chilli powder	1 teaspoon (optional)
garam masala	1 teaspoon

Melt the ghee, and fry the onion until golden brown with the garlic, ginger, cinnamon stick, cloves, cardamom pods and ground cummin. This will take about 10 minutes, if you keep the heat fairly low, and stir occasionally to prevent sticking.

Add the meat and cook for several minutes, turning frequently.

Now add the yoghurt and chilli powder (if used). Cover, and simmer very gently for about 35 minutes, until the meat is tender.

Sprinkle the garam masala and the mint over, cover, and leave for 5 minutes before serving.

This is not a 'toned-down' curry, but a rather special dish which the whole family can enjoy while introducing the children to spicy food. The chilli powder is not at all necessary, unless the children want to develop their palates, with a view to venturing into the other sections in Ali's menu!

– – – – –

CHICKEN CURRY (2)

chicken	4 portions
onions	8oz/250g finely sliced
turmeric	½ teaspoon
ground cardamom (black)	½ teaspoon
ground cummin	½ teaspoon
chilli powder	½ teaspoon
cloves	3
cinnamon	1" piece of stick
garlic	2 cloves, crushed and finely chopped
salt	1½ teaspoons
freshly ground black pepper	to taste
ghee or butter	3 tablespoons
water or stock	½ pint/300ml
yoghurt	3 tablespoons
tomato puree	1 tablespoon
sugar	pinch

Melt the ghee or butter, and add the turmeric, cardamom, cummin, chilli powder, cloves, cinnamon, salt and pepper. Fry for several minutes, stirring occasionally.

Add the onions and garlic and continue cooking over a gentle heat, stirring frequently, for 10 minutes.

Place the chicken pieces in the pan and fry for 5 minutes on each side, taking care not to burn them. Add the yoghurt, tomato puree, sugar and water or stock. Blend in well.

Cover the pan, and simmer gently for 30 - 40 minutes, until the chicken is cooked through and tender. Allow it to stand off the heat for 5 minutes before serving.

— — ▬ — —

LASSI

Try a childrens' version of the drink Lassi. For each serving, place 2 tablespoons of natural yoghurt in a tumbler with 2 teaspoons of sugar, top with soda and stir thoroughly.

SUNDRIES

CHAPATIS

PARATHA

TANDOORI NAN

RATIA

SPICED ONION

PAPADAM

MINT & YOGHURT CHUTNEY

SPECIAL ONION SALAD

CHAPATIS

fine wholemeal flour or roti flour	10oz/280g
salt	1½ teaspoons
lukewarm water	8 fl oz/220ml
ghee or oil	1 tablespoon

Sift the flour with the salt into a mixing bowl, tip in the water and mix to a soft dough. Turn onto a floured board and knead for ten minutes. Put the dough back into the bowl, cover with clear plastic, or a damp cloth, and leave for 1 hour or more if possible.

To cook the chapatis, pull off a piece of dough about the size of a ping pong ball, place on a lightly floured board, and roll out as thinly as possible into a circular shape. Heat a griddle, or heavy based frying pan, and cook the chapatis one at a time of the hot surface, leaving for about one minute on each side. If you press the chapatis lightly around the edges with a fish slice as they are cooking, it encourages bubbles to form.

Wrap the warm chapatis in a clean cloth until ready to serve. Make sure you have some butter on the table!

— — — — —

PARATHA (makes 8 - 10)

roti, or white flour	6oz/168g
fine wholemeal flour	6oz/168g
salt	1½ teaspoons
ghee or butter	6oz/168g
water	8 fl oz/220 ml

Sift the flours with the salt, and rub in 1oz/30g (or 1 tablespoon) of the ghee or butter. Pour in the water and mix to a soft dough.

Cover with clear plastic or a damp cloth, and leave for about an hour.

With regard to the use of ghee or butter in the recipe, note that if you use butter, when you melt it you will get a slight froth on the top. Remove this carefully, and liquid oil underneath will be clarified butter, or ghee! This being so, I will no longer use the word 'butter', with reference to parathas.

Allow yourself about 30 minutes to roll and cook the parathas. Divide the dough into 10 portions. Roll each into a ball, then, roll each ball into a circular shape and as thinly as possible. Brush it generously with the melted ghee. Make a cut from the centre to the edge, then roll up from one cut edge into a cone shape. Hold the cone up on its point with one hand, place your other fist over the top and squash it down. Now roll it out again, but not as thinly as the first time. Brush it liberally with ghee, brush your frying pan, or griddle with ghee, place the paratha on the heated surface, dry side down. After a minute, turn it over, and brush the side now facing you with more ghee. Continue to turn, and brush with ghee until the paratha is golden brown on both sides. Place on a plate, or in a basket, and cover with a cloth until you are ready to serve them.

This may sound time-consuming, but you can be supervising other dishes at the same time, preparatory to serving up your meal.

— — — — —

TANDOORI NAN

plain flour	10oz/280g
baking powder	4 teaspoon
caster sugar	1 tablespoon
egg	1
milk (or buttermilk)	½ pint/150ml
salt	pinch
cooking oil	2 tablespoons
butter	1 tablespoon melted
sesame seeds	2 teaspoons

Sift the flour, baking powder and salt, and stir in the sugar.

Beat the egg and milk together, and pour into the flour. Mix to a soft dough. Knead well, then divide the dough into three pieces and shape into buns. Place them on a well greased baking sheet, brush thickly with oil, cover with a damp cloth and leave overnight if possible. The longer you leave them to stand, up to 24 hours, the lighter they will be. Try to keep the cloth damp during the standing period.

The nearest I have been able to get to the effect of cooking in the Tandoor is to pre-heat the grill leaving the grill pan under the grill. Take one piece of dough, and flatten it between your hands. Pass it back and forth from hand to hand until it begins to stretch under its own weight. You can cheat a bit and stretch it yourself, but once its diameter is greater than that of your hands it will stretch itself, believe me. It will also become thinner, quite naturally.

When it resembles a large, thin, wobbly pancake, brush one side with oil and place that side on the hot grill pan, about 4" away form the element. Keep a close eye on it. within 2 minutes it should have puffed up and started to brown in places. By the time the highest peaks on your Nan are dark brown, it will be cooked through. Whip it out immediately!

Brush the top with melted butter, and sprinkle with sesame seeds. Eat as soon as possible.

If, by any strange chance, you can't manage to finish off three of these at one sitting, either freeze the remaining dough, or cook it for breakfast the next day.

— — — —

RATIA

yoghurt (plain or natural)	5 fl oz/142ml
cucumber, onion or	
cooked potato	3 tablespoons, diced
lemon juice	1 teaspoon
salt	pinch
cayenne pepper or chilli powder .	¼ teaspoon (to taste)

Mix the vegetable of your choice with the yoghurt, lemon juice and salt, and sprinkle the cayenne or chilli powder over the top.

SPICED ONION

onion	8oz finely sliced
tomato sauce	2½ tablespoons
tomato puree	2 teaspoons
chilli powder	½ teaspoon
salt	scant ½ teaspoon (to taste)

Blend the tomato sauce, tomato puree, chilli powder and salt well. Add the onion and toss well in the sauce. Cover, and leave for 30 minutes before serving.

— — — —

PAPADAM

These are spiced lentil wafers which are obtainable from most supermarkets in packets. They come in the form of dry, flat discs.

To prepare them, drop them one at a time into hot oil for a few seconds only, turning once. They will puff up very quickly and turn golden brown. Drain them by standing them up edgewise on absorbent paper.

— — — —

MINT & YOGHURT CHUTNEY

yoghurt (plain or natural)	5 fl oz/142ml
tomato sauce	2 tablespoons
sugar	1 teaspoon
chilli powder	½ teaspoon (to taste)
mint	1 teaspoon dried, or 1 tablespoon fresh, chopped

Mix all the ingredients together thoroughly, and preferably an hour before required.

Serve with any Tandoori, or Tikka dish.

SPECIAL ONION SALAD

lettuce	small head
onion	4oz/125g
tomatoes	4oz/125g
cucumber	4oz/125g
salt	pinch
lemon juice	2 tablespoons

Hold the washed lettuce leaves together in a bundle in your hand, place them on the chopping board, and slice across.

Slice the onion and tomato fairly thickly also — about ¼" slices. Slice the cucumber the same way, then cut all the slices into ¼" strips.

Toss the ingredients in a bowl, sprinkle the salt and lemon juice over just before serving.

SWEETS

FERNAI

GULAB JAMIN

KHEER (Cream Rice)

FERNAI

milk	1½ pints/860ml
ground rice	2 tablespoons
sugar	2 tablespoons (to taste)
rose essence	2 drops
almonds (blanched)	2 teaspoons, chopped
pistachio nuts	2 teaspoons, chopped finely

Mix the ground rice and sugar to a cream with a tablespoon or two of the milk.

Bring the rest of the milk to the boil, stir in the rice cream and continue to cook over a low heat, stirring constantly, until the mixture thickens. Add the rose essence.

Remove from the heat, and pour into a serving dish (or individual dishes). Decorate with the almonds and pistachio nuts.

— — ▬ ▬ —

GULAB JAMIN

Ostermilk (dried baby milk) . . .	6oz/185g
sugar	6oz/185g
water	1 pint/600ml
egg	1 beaten
butter	6oz/185g
plain flour	2 teaspoons
green cardamom	4 using the seeds only
self raising flour	2 teaspoons

First, prepare the sugar syrup. Place the sugar and water in a saucepan, and bring to the boil very slowly, stirring until the sugar is completely dissolved. Leave it to simmer gently while you prepare the rest of the ingredients.

Mix the Ostermilk with the plain flour, self raising flour, cardamom seeds and beaten egg, until you have a light dough.

Heat the butter in a small saucepan, shape pieces of the dough into balls, or small sausage shapes, and fry them in the hot butter, turning carefully to ensure browning. When they are cooked through drain them thoroughly, and place them in the hot sugar syrup for about 30 minutes.

Serve them hot, with ice cream — a delicious combination!

– – – – –

KHEER (Cream Rice)

milk	1½ pints/860ml
round grain (pudding) rice	4oz/125g
sugar	2 tablespoons (to taste)
sultanas	2 teaspoons
water	1 teacup

Place the milk in a large frying pan, and bring it to the boil. Reduce the heat, and continue to boil gently, stirring constantly, until you have reduced it by half. This will take about 20 minutes, and you must stir all the time, to avoid burning the milk at the bottom of the pan.

Pour the ¾ pint condensed milk which you have just prepared into a saucepan, add the rice and water, and cook over a low heat until the rice is soft. You will need to stir this quite often to keep it smooth.

Now add the sugar, to taste, and the sultanas, and cook for a further 2 minutes.